Blue Banner Biography

Brett Favre

Heidi Krumenauer

Mitchell Lane
PUBLISHERS

P.O. Box 196
Hockessin, Delaware 19707
Visit us on the web: www.mitchelllane.com
Comments? email us: mitchelllane@mitchelllane.com

Mitchell Lane PUBLISHERS

Printing   2   3   4   5   6   7   8   9

Blue Banner Biographies

Library of Congress Cataloging-in-Publication Data
Krumenauer, Heidi.
  Brett Favre / by Heidi Krumenauer.
    p. cm. — (Blue banner biographies)
  Includes bibliographical references and index.
  ISBN 978-1-58415-670-3 (library bound)
  1. Favre, Brett—Juvenile literature. 2. Football players—United States—Biography—Juvenile literature. 3. Quarterbacks (Football)—United States—Biography—Juvenile literature. I. Title.
  GV939.F29K78 2009
  796.332092—dc22
  [B]
                                                                                2008008053

ABOUT THE AUTHOR: Heidi Krumenauer began writing newspaper articles as a teenager. She continues to write in addition to working full-time in management with a Fortune 400 insurance company. She has written more than 1,000 articles and has contributed chapters to eight books. Her first book, *Why Does Grandma Have a Wibble?*, was released in 2007. She is also the author of *Rihanna* and *Sean Kingston* for Mitchell Lane Publishers. Heidi and her husband, Jeff, are raising their two sons, Noah and Payton, in Southern Wisconsin.

PUBLISHER'S NOTE: The following story has been thoroughly researched, and to the best of our knowledge represents a true story. While every possible effort has been made to ensure accuracy, the publisher will not assume liability for damages caused by inaccuracies in the data and makes no warranty on the accuracy of the information contained herein. This story has not been authorized or endorsed by Brett Favre.

Blue Banner Biography

Considered one of the greatest sports heroes of all time, Brett Favre started playing professional football with the Atlanta Falcons in 1991, but after that season he spent most of the rest of his career with the Green Bay Packers. He said in October 2005: "If you do what you're asked to do, and you're good at what you do, success will come. You won't have to go find it. It'll come to you."

Time to Hang Up the Jersey?

There were worried faces in the stadium—some of them showing signs of sadness and tears. As Brett Favre walked off the turf of Soldier Field in Chicago, Illinois, on December 31, 2006, he saluted the crowd. Football fans everywhere wondered if they had just witnessed Favre's final game in the NFL. If it was his last game, he had played it with the same style that his fans and his competitors were accustomed to— with grace and gusto! The Green Bay Packers quarterback passed for 285 yards and threw for one touchdown. The 26-7 win over the Chicago Bears raised his team's overall record against the Bears to 22-7. The victory, however, wasn't enough for the Packers to secure a playoff game. Their season was finished and, according to Favre, his career was probably finished, too.

Following the game, thirty-seven-year-old Favre gave a tearful interview on national television, hinting that he was strongly considering retirement from his memorable football career of sixteen years. Nobody wanted to believe that the man who led the Packers out of a long losing slump was ready to hang up his #4 jersey. The only man with an answer was Favre, and he told the press he wasn't going to make the decision for a couple of weeks.

Favre loved playing football, and he loved the Packers, but he was frustrated. Ending the 2006 season with a record of 8-8, he wasn't happy. Besides that, he was struggling with changes within the Packers organization and problems with the team's offense. He took the blame for some of the problems, admitting that even though he was still strong and healthy, he wasn't making the big plays like he should. Favre told ESPN's Chris Mortensen in 2006, "I love the game too much and I love my legacy too much to have that just be OK, and I don't want to be OK. I want to be good, and I don't know if I'm committed enough [right now] to be good on an everyday basis." The man who doubted his NFL commitment was the same man who just nine years earlier had put Green Bay, Wisconsin, back on the map.

> After only five seasons as the starting quarterback for the Packers, Favre led his team to the one place Packers fans wanted to go—Super Bowl XXXI!

The Packers had suffered through more than twenty years of failing seasons. Green Bay fans are loyal, but they were tired of losing. They were hopeful that some magic would be sprinkled on historic Lambeau Field, so they, too, might experience the joy of being part of a Super Bowl team. That dream seemed far away until Brett Favre stepped onto the field in 1992. At twenty-two years old and with an arm that shot footballs like cannonballs, Favre was exactly what the failing team needed. And after only five seasons as the starting quarterback for the Packers, Favre led his team to the one place Packers fans wanted to go—Super Bowl XXXI!

On January 26, 1997, Favre stepped out onto the AstroTurf of the Louisiana Superdome in New Orleans in front of 72,301 screaming fans. He'd heard the cheers before, and he'd seen the sea of yellow Cheeseheads in the crowd, but that night was different. It was the Super Bowl—a dream come true for Favre and every Packer fan!

Under the big lights and the cameras, Favre completed 14 of 27 passes and threw for two touchdown passes. On only the second play of the game, he threw a 54-yard touchdown pass to Andre Rison. Later in the game, he threw an 81-yard pass to Antonio Freeman for another touchdown. Under the leadership of their quarterback, the Green Bay Packers defeated the New England Patriots 35-21.

Only one year later, on January 25, 1998, the Packers were back in the championship game. This time, Brett and his

The Cheesehead, worn by this diehard fan in 2006, is a foam hat in the shape of a cheese wedge. Because Wisconsin is known for its cheese production, the Cheesehead has become the proud symbol of many loyal Packers fans.

teammates were in San Diego's Qualcomm Stadium in California for Super Bowl XXXII against the Denver Broncos. He had 25 completions in 42 attempts and threw for only 256 yards. Favre's performance wasn't terrible, but it was considered average. Average doesn't win the Super Bowl. The Broncos won 31-24.

After publicly considering retirement following the 2006 season, Favre announced early in 2007 that he was going stick around for another year.

Maybe it didn't matter how great Favre's game was; Denver was prepared to win. Broncos cornerback Ray Crockett watched hours of game tape to learn Favre's style of play. "We saw how many chances he takes," he said. "He's succeeded on most of those chances the last few years and gained tremendous confidence. By being a risk-taker, he's become the greatest quarterback in the game. But what made him great got him in trouble against us."

Win or lose, Favre was exactly what the Packers needed. And no matter when he would decide to retire, he would be doing it in Green Bay. On March 1, 2001, he signed a lifetime contract with the Packers— meaning it would be in effect until after 2010. "I enjoy it here. I don't want to move. I enjoy the fans and I just want to stay. I couldn't envision myself playing for another team," he said.

After publicly considering retirement following the 2006 season, Favre announced early in 2007 that he was going to stick around for another year. No doubt, he was happy with his decision. During the 2007 season, he led the Packers to a 13-3 record with 4,155 passing yards and 28 touchdowns. His quarterback rating was 95.7, the best in 11 seasons. In

With hopes of returning to his third Super Bowl, Favre's dreams were dashed when the New York Giants defeated the Packers in the NFC Championship game on January 20, 2008. His last play of the game was intercepted.

September, he broke Dan Marino's NFL touchdown pass record (420). Even more exciting, he led the Packers to within one game of the Super Bowl!

On January 20, 2008, the Packers played against the New York Giants for the NFC Championship game in Green Bay. With temperatures dipping well below zero, Favre played in his coldest game ever — the third coldest game in NFL history. In overtime, Giants kicker Lawrence Tynes kicked a 47-yard field goal, winning the game 23-20 and shattering Favre's dreams of another Super Bowl. Still, his super season proved that Favre had the athletic and mental ability to be a team leader. After seventeen seasons, he still didn't look like a guy who was ready to hang up his jersey.

Legend Raised in the South

*B*rett Lorenzo Favre was born to Bonita and Irvin Favre on October 10, 1969. Weighing in at 9 pounds, 15 ounces, it wasn't a surprise to his family that he would grow up to be 6 feet 2 inches tall and 230 pounds.

Brett, of French and Choctaw (Native American) descent, was born in Gulfport, Mississippi, and grew up outside the small town of Kiln (pronounced KILL), Mississippi. At age three, he received his first football uniform (helmet and pads included). Though no one expected it, that uniform would be the first of many uniforms to hang in Brett's locker over the next few decades.

As a child, Brett hung out with his best friends—his older brother, Scott, and younger brother, Jeff, on his family's 52-acre backwoods property. The Favres didn't have neighbors that lived close by, so Brett and his siblings usually only played with each other. Although they had a younger sister, Brandi, Brett and his brothers were always together, fishing, swimming in the bayou, hunting in the woods, and playing football and baseball. According to their mother, Bonita, the boys always had something in their hands—something they

Brett learned a lot from his high school coach and father, "Big Irv." As a quarterback for Hancock North Central High, Brett wasn't often allowed to show his passing talent. Because Irv liked to run plays that would use the talents of his running backs, Brett rarely threw more than five passes in a game.

could throw, like rocks, potatoes, or balls made of duct tape. And they were always dirty from long days of playing outside.

As Brett grew up there was only one girl who could compete with his brothers—Deanna Tynes. Brett met Deanna in kindergarten, and they loved playing ball together. At age fourteen, the two started dating, but Brett was never too distracted by his love life. He was very serious about sports.

> *Even though Brett showed early signs of athletic ability on the football field, he seemed to shine more on the baseball field.*

The Favre boys were natural athletes. Because their father was the high school football coach, the boys spent a lot of time on the football field. Each of them played the quarterback position, mostly because Big Irv, as their father was widely known, was the head coach at Hancock North Central High. Irv didn't let his sons get away with anything. He had the same high expectations of them as he did of the rest of the players. Irv was a strict, commanding man. Brett's brother Jeff said, "Dad was hard on everybody. He'd run a lot of people off the team. He didn't put up with much, that's for sure."

Brett was very strong and had the ability to make a great linebacker, but Irv needed him as a quarterback. Often there weren't enough kids on the practice field. Irv made sure there was always a quarterback by relying on his son.

Even though Brett showed early signs of athletic ability on the football field, he seemed to shine more on the baseball field. He started playing baseball for the high school team as an eighth-grader and continued to play through his senior year, earning five varsity letters. Opposing teams feared Brett because his pitches were so fierce. Bonita said of her son, "There were kids who wouldn't bat against him because he threw so hard." During one game he threw the ball so hard it shot past first base, cleared the dugout, flew through an open window on the opposing team's bus, and bounced around inside.

On the football field, however, Brett rarely got the chance to show his strength. Irv didn't want the quarterbacks throwing more than five passes in each game. That strategy almost cost Brett a shot with the University of Southern Mississippi. Irv begged Southern Miss to send someone to look at his son in action. The only problem was that Brett didn't get enough action when Southern Miss offensive line coach Mark McHale came to town. He threw a couple of passes, but that wasn't enough to impress the coach. Irv promised him more action if he'd return the next week to watch Brett. Six or seven passes was all he had, but it must have been enough. Brett received a scholarship to play with Southern Miss following his senior year at Hancock.

Six or seven passes was all he had, but it must have been enough. Brett received a scholarship to play with Southern Miss following his senior year at Hancock.

From Southern Miss to the NFL

Southern Miss was the only major university to offer Brett a scholarship. He was recruited as a defensive back, but as a freshman in the fall of 1987, seventeen-year-old Brett took over as the team's quarterback. He had expected to sit on the bench for much of the season, but that changed during the third quarter of game three. Coach Jim Carmody, who was upset with the offense, called Brett to the field. Once Brett started playing, the stands went wild. Chris McGee, a senior wide receiver and team cocaptain, said, "I thought somebody in the stands got to fighting or something. The next thing we know, uncharacteristic of our head coach, we start throwing the football all over the field." With two touchdown passes, Brett led his team to a come-from-behind, 31-24 victory. That was just the beginning of what he would do for his team over the next four years.

Brett's college years were impressive. During his four years as a Golden Eagle, he led his team to 29 victories and two bowl games. He set a few school records along the way, too: passing yards (8,193), pass attempts (1,234), completions (656), passing percentage (53.0), and touchdowns (55). He

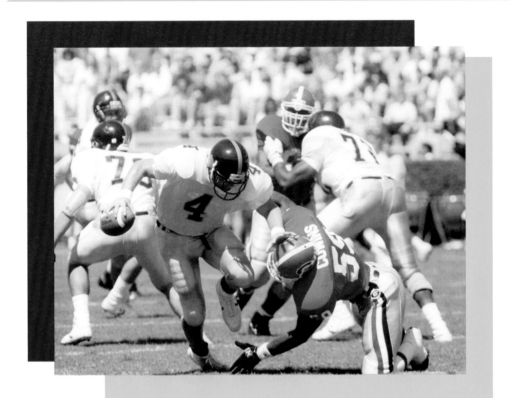

On September 15, 1990, while playing for Southern Mississippi, Brett was dragged to the ground by Georgia Bulldogs linebacker Norman Cowins. Just a few weeks earlier, on July 14, Brett was involved in a near-fatal car accident near his home, and doctors had to remove 30 inches of his small intestine. It didn't take him long to recover and get back out on the field.

had only 35 interceptions. Twenty years later, Brett was still ranked as one of the best players in NCAA history. When it came time to pursue a career after college, the NFL was a perfect fit for Brett.

Favre made his debut in the NFL on October 27, 1991, with the Atlanta Falcons. He was a second-round draft pick and thirty-third pick overall. His preseason play was much more impressive than the regular season. Even though his performance was not remarkable, he completed 14 of 32 passes for 160 yards and two touchdowns in the preseason.

In 1991, Favre played his first NFL season with the Atlanta Falcons, but he didn't complete a single pass with them. He made his first NFL completion as a Green Bay Packer on September 13, 1992 – which he threw to himself! The pass was deflected by the opposing team and Favre caught the ball, but lost seven yards.

During the regular season with the Falcons, he was active for only three games; he played in only two of them. He didn't pass for any touchdowns. In fact, he didn't even complete one pass! Favre's first NFL season started poorly, but someone had seen promise in the young rookie one year earlier during his college days. After only one season with the Falcons, Favre traded in his black-and-red Falcons uniform for a green-and-gold one instead.

On February 10, 1992, Green Bay Packers General Manager Ron Wolf traded a first-round draft selection for a quarterback who would back up starter Don "Majik" Majkowski. Even Favre wasn't prepared for how fast he would take on a larger role with the team. During the season's third game, Majik suffered an ankle injury. Favre moved to the field to replace the injured quarterback in the first quarter of the game. He took charge and led the Packers to a come-from-behind 24-23 victory over the Cincinnati Bengals. In his first year as a starting quarterback, Favre finished the season 8-5. He also set two Green Bay passing records. To top off a successful season, he was named to the NFC Pro Bowl team alongside quarterback legends Steve Young and Troy Aikman. At age twenty-three, he was the youngest quarterback at that time to play in an AFC-NFC Pro Bowl.

> *In his first year as a starting quarterback, Favre finished the 1992 season 8-5. He also set two Green Bay passing records.*

Even Heroes Have Their Struggles

For a man who has been featured on the cover of *Sports Illustrated* more than a dozen times and owns two Super Bowl rings, it would be easy to assume Brett Favre's life is perfect in every area. Favre will quickly say that not even he can escape the troubles that life can throw your way. While he has endured plenty of bitter battles on the football field, none have compared to the ones he has faced in his personal life.

After a few years of hard hits and painful injuries on the field, Favre was depending on painkillers to help him get through the day. In May of 1996, he publicly admitted his addiction to painkillers and then later discussed his specific addiction to the prescription drug Vicodin. In his May press conference, twenty-six-year-old Favre sat with girlfriend Deanna Tynes and Packers coach Mike Holmgren by his side. Trying to find the right words, Favre told the press, "I'm 26 years old. I just threw 38 touchdown passes in one year, and I'm the NFL MVP. People look at me and say, 'I'd love to be that guy.' But if they knew what it took to be that guy, they wouldn't love to be him, I can guarantee you that." Following his press conference, Favre entered the Menninger

Clinic in Topeka, Kansas, where he stayed and attended group therapy sessions for forty-six days.

Favre's problem with painkillers began in one of his first games with the Packers. On November 15, 1992, Favre suffered a separated left shoulder after being sacked by Reggie White, who was playing for the Philadelphia Eagles. Having joined the team only eight weeks earlier, Favre didn't want Coach Holmgren to know how badly he was hurting. After winning the game against the Eagles, Favre asked the team doctor for a painkiller. "Some players take it and get sick to their stomach, so they don't do it again," Favre wrote in his 1997 autobiography *Favre: For the Record.* "Other players think it feels pretty good but they'd never take it enough to get addicted. Then there are players like me, who take it and get hooked."

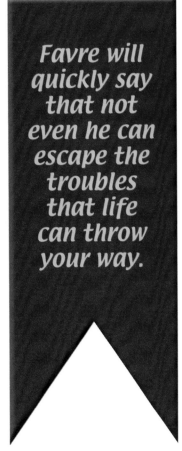

Favre will quickly say that not even he can escape the troubles that life can throw your way.

One Vicodin turned to two—and then two turned to three a day. By the end of 1994, Favre was popping up to fifteen pills a day. His health was suffering. Following an ankle surgery in February 1996, he suffered a seizure. That was the final straw! Doctors and NFL personnel confronted him about his addiction. A few months later, he was entering a substance-abuse center in Topeka, Kansas.

As Favre came to grips with his addiction, he also reflected on his life. In June, he proposed to Deanna, who had been his girlfriend for twelve years. They were married in July just before the start of Packers training camp.

After dating for twelve years, Brett and Deanna Tynes were married on July 14, 1996, at St. Agnes Catholic Church in Green Bay. Also pictured are Deanna's mother (left) and Brett's mother, Bonita (right).

During a press conference following his treatment, Favre said of his recovery, "Believe me when I tell you that this is going to be hard, but I have faced tougher trials and succeeded. I will not allow myself to be defeated by this challenge." Brett has stayed true to his word. Painkiller addiction became a thing of his past, but personal challenges have not.

Brett was especially close to his father, Irv. One of the most memorable games for Brett—and for his fans—was a Monday Night Football game against the Oakland Raiders on December 22, 2003. Only twenty-four hours earlier, fifty-eight-year-old Irv passed away from a sudden heart attack while driving near Kiln. Brett learned of his father's death, but he didn't leave his team. He stayed in Oakland to play the game. Many said, and Favre would most likely agree, that it was one of his most memorable games. Grieving the loss of his father, he threw four touchdown passes in the first quarter and had 399 totals yards in the game, leading the Packers to a 41-7 victory over the Raiders.

Only one year later, Favre's emotional strength was tested again. Deanna was diagnosed with breast cancer in October 2004, just four days after her younger brother was killed in an ATV accident. On October 22, Deanna underwent a successful surgery in New York. She told *USA Today* of Brett, "I don't think I could have done it without him. We're just trying to find something good in all of the bad and find a way to make it better."

Brett struggled with his wife's cancer. He said, "I still look at her as the girl I was chasing around in eighth grade. And when Dad passed away and her brother passed away and she got cancer, you go, 'What happened? We're still kids. Kids are not supposed to get cancer. Kids are not supposed to see their younger brother get killed.'"

When Deanna started losing her hair from the chemotherapy, Brett showed his support by allowing his teammates to shave his head, too.

When Deanna started losing her hair from the chemotherapy, Brett showed his support by allowing his teammates to shave his head, too. He also spent a lot of time reading about cancer. Brett helped to establish the Deanna Favre Hope Foundation, which provides financial help to women with breast cancer.

Meanwhile, Brett never gave up on the game. Former Packers head coach Mike Sherman said, "Any man would

Brett and Deanna Favre join First Lady Laura Bush as she cuts the ribbon to open a new playground at Hancock North Central Elementary School in Kiln, Mississippi. Kiln was severely damaged when Hurricane Katrina ripped through the town in 2005. KaBOOM!, a nonprofit organization, began Operation Playground to replace playgrounds across the Gulf Coast.

have to contemplate his future when his wife is fighting cancer, [but] . . . he never lost his enthusiasm for the game."

Deanna's cancer was not the last tragedy for Brett. In August 2005, he learned that his childhood home on the Mississippi Gulf Coast had been destroyed by flood damage caused by Hurricane Katrina. In the middle of the crisis, Favre waited for two days to hear from his family. When his family finally reached him by phone, they told him his childhood home would need to be bulldozed. Brett and Deanna's home in Hattiesburg, Mississippi, was not impacted by the storm. Instead, it became a place of refuge for more than fifty of Brett and Deanna's family members and friends.

The End of an Era

March 4, 2008, was a day that all Packers fans dreaded. Packers General Manager Ted Thompson announced that Brett Favre had made his decision to retire. Two days later, on March 6, Favre addressed the public in a very tearful and emotional press conference.

Favre had talked about retirement many times, but it seemed he might never make that official announcement. With graying hair, sore feet, and squeaking joints, Favre was considered an old man by professional standards, but he still put every ounce of energy he had into the game of football. And even with a few physical ailments, he was known as an ironman to his teammates and opponents.

With serious injuries—including a concussion, separated shoulder, broken thumb, severe bruises, and sprains—Favre played every game since starting his career with the Packers on September 27, 1992. In fact, while injured, he led his team to many victories. In a game against the New York Giants on October 3, 2004, Favre suffered a concussion. Without medical clearance from the team doctors, he returned to the field to throw a touchdown pass. In 2003, with a broken thumb, he threw three touchdowns for a critical 23-20 win over the Minnesota Vikings. And the list goes on.

On the field, Favre was a leader. Off the field, he has been no different. In 1996, he founded the Brett Favre Fourward Foundation, which provides aid to disadvantaged children in Wisconsin, the place he played football, and Mississippi, the place he still calls home. Each year, Favre's golf tournaments, celebrity softball games, and fund-raising dinners, along with other money collected through his foundation, raises money for children's charities.

When making decisions about his future, Brett consults with his wife and two daughters, Brittany and Breleigh.

In 2007, Favre partnered with Wrangler Jeans to benefit many children. The jean company promised to donate 100 pairs of jeans for every touchdown pass that Favre threw in the 2007 season. He threw 28 touchdown passes. Multiply that by 100 pairs of jeans, and you have 2,800 very happy girls and boys!

Favre has also been a strong supporter of other charities, including Special Olympics, Make-A-Wish Foundation, Easter Seals of Wisconsin, and Cerebral Palsy of Wisconsin.

More than anything, Favre has been a strong supporter of his family. When making decisions about his future, he consults with his wife and two daughters, Brittany and Breleigh. No doubt, he consulted with them when he made the decision to walk away from the game that made him a football icon.

Favre presents a check for $20,000 to Janice Baddley, president and CEO of Make-A-Wish Foundation of Mississippi. The money, raised by the Brett Favre Fourward Foundation, would benefit the Mississippi Special Olympics.

Wiping his eyes in the sixty-seven-minute press conference, thirty-eight-year-old Favre shared his reasons for retirement. "I've given everything I possibly could give to this organization . . . to the game of football. I don't think I've got anything left to give," he said. "I know I can play. But I don't think I want to, and that's what it really comes down to." He admitted he was physically able to play another year, but added, "It's been a great career for me, and it's over. As hard as that is for me to say, it's over."

Favre runs the ball during week two of the 2008 season — his first as a New York Jet.

Even after his heartfelt good-bye, as soon as training camp started, Favre got the itch to play again. He asked to return to the Packers as their starting quarterback, but he and the Packers could not reach an agreement. The resulting battle between Favre and Green Bay's front office was covered in depth by reporters, and it became an embarrassing spectacle for both parties. Finally they made a complicated trade, and Favre was signed with the New York Jets.

With Favre's strong arm and unrivaled playmaking ability, the Jets' running game exploded. In week ten, the Jets demolished the St. Louis Rams, winning by 44 points, the highest point difference in team history. The confidence Favre brought to the team, and the amount of focus he demanded from opponents, made the Jets not only play better, but playoff bound. The end of one era signaled the beginning of a new one.

CAREER STATS

YEAR	TEAM	G	GS	Comp	Att	Pct	Yds	Avg	TD	Int	Rate
2007	Green Bay Packers	16	16	356	535	66.5	4,155	7.8	28	15	95.7
2006	Green Bay Packers	16	16	343	613	56.0	3,885	6.3	18	18	72.7
2005	Green Bay Packers	16	16	372	607	61.3	3,881	6.4	20	29	70.9
2004	Green Bay Packers	16	16	346	540	64.1	4,088	7.6	30	17	92.4
2003	Green Bay Packers	16	16	308	471	65.4	3,361	7.1	32	21	90.4
2002	Green Bay Packers	16	16	341	551	61.9	3,658	6.6	27	16	85.6
2001	Green Bay Packers	16	16	314	510	61.6	3,921	7.7	32	15	94.1
2000	Green Bay Packers	16	16	338	580	58.3	3,812	6.6	20	16	78.0
1999	Green Bay Packers	16	16	341	595	57.3	4,091	6.9	22	23	74.7
1998	Green Bay Packers	16	16	347	551	63.0	4,212	7.6	31	23	87.8
1997	Green Bay Packers	16	16	304	513	59.3	3,867	7.5	35	16	92.6
1996	Green Bay Packers	16	16	325	543	59.9	3,899	7.2	39	13	95.8
1995	Green Bay Packers	16	16	359	570	63.0	4,413	7.7	38	13	99.5
1994	Green Bay Packers	16	16	363	582	62.4	3,882	6.7	33	14	90.7
1993	Green Bay Packers	16	16	318	522	60.9	3,303	6.3	19	24	72.2
1992	Green Bay Packers	15	13	302	471	64.1	3,227	6.9	18	13	85.3
1991	Atlanta Falcons	2	0	0	4	0.0	0	0.0	0	2	0.0
TOTAL				5,377	8,758	61.4	61,655	7.0	442	288	85.7

(G=Games, GS=Games started, Comp=Completions, Att=Attempts, Pct=Percentage, Yds=Yards, Avg=Average, TD=Touchdown, Int=Interceptions, Rate=Quarterback rating)

1969 Brett Lorenzo Favre is born to Irvin and Bonita Favre in Gulfport, Mississippi, on October 10.

1979 In fifth grade, Brett first plays quarterback for Pee Wee youth football.

1982 As an eighth-grader, Brett is a pitcher on the high school's varsity baseball team.

1987 Brett graduates from Hancock North Central and starts his freshman year at the University of Southern Mississippi.

1989 Brett's daughter, Brittany, is born on February 6.

1990 One month after having 30 inches of his small intestine removed following a car accident, Brett helps his team, the Southern Mississippi Golden Eagles, pull off a historical comeback win against the Crimson Tide.

1991 Brett graduates from Southern Miss. He is selected as a second-round draft pick (33rd overall) by the Atlanta Falcons. In his first regular season, Brett is 0-4 in pass completions.

1992 Green Bay Packers General Manager Ron Wolf trades a #1 draft pick for 22-year-old Brett. At 23 years old, Brett earns a spot on the NFL Pro Bowl as the youngest quarterback in NFL history.

1993 Hancock North Central retires Brett's high school jersey — #10.

1996 Favre enters the NFL's substance abuse program to deal with his addiction to painkillers. After dating for more than 12 years, he and Deanna Tynes marry. Brett starts the Brett Favre Fourward Foundation, aiding underprivileged children in Wisconsin and Mississippi. After setting an NFC single-season record with 38 touchdown passes and leading the NFL with 4,413 yards, Favre wins the MVP award.

1997 In Super Bowl XXXI, Favre and the Packers enjoy a victory of 35-21 over the New England Patriots. Favre is inducted into the Southern Miss Sports Hall of Fame. His autobiography, *Favre: For the Record,* is published.

1998 In their second championship game in a row, Super Bowl XXXII, the Green Bay Packers come up short, losing to the Denver Broncos.

1999 Breleigh Favre is born to Brett and Deanna on July 13.

2001 Favre signs a 10-year, $100 million contract (an NFL record) with the Packers.

2002 He is named NFL Player of the Year by *Sports Illustrated*.

2003 His father, Big Irv, dies on December 21 after a heart attack. Brett surprises his teammates by playing in the matchup against Oakland the next evening. He stuns the nation when he passes for 399 yards and four touchdowns, moving into second place in NFL history for career TD passes while leading the Packers to a 41-7 victory during Monday Night Football.

2004 Deanna is diagnosed with breast cancer. Wisconsin Governor Jim Doyle declares November 29, 2004, as Brett Favre Day to honor his 200th consecutive NFL start. Brett helps his wife establish the Deanna Favre Hope Foundation for women with breast cancer.

2005 Hurricane Katrina destroys his childhood home.

2006 An emotional ending to a game against the Seattle Seahawks on December 31 leaves fans wondering whether Brett will return for another season.

2007 Brett is named *Sports Illustrated* Sportsman of the Year. On September 30, he becomes the NFL leader in touchdown passes (421), beating former quarterback Dan Marino's record.

2008 Brett and the Packers play in their first NFC Championship since 1998, losing in overtime, 23-20. Brett is named the 2007 FedEx Air Player of the Year. On March 4, General Manager Ted Thompson announces that Favre will retire from the NFL. Favre has second thoughts and comes back out of retirement. On August 6, he signs with the New York Jets.

Books

Carlson, Chuck. *Brett Favre: America's Quarterback.* Chicago: Triumph Books, 2007.

Kertscher, Tom. *Brett Favre: A Packer Fan's Tribute.* Nashville, Tennessee: Cumberland House Publishing, 2008.

Nelson, Ted W. *Brett Favre (Sports Heroes).* Minneapolis: Capstone, 2001.

Thornley, Stew. *Brett Favre (Super Sports Star).* Berkeley Heights, New Jersey: Enslow Elementary, 2003.

Works Consulted

D'Amato, Gary. "200 Reasons to Admire Favre." JSOnline.com, *Milwaukee Journal Sentinel*, November 28, 2004. http://www.jsonline.com/story/index.aspx?id=279432

———. "Drug Abuse Rocks His World. JSOnline, *Milwaukee Journal Sentinel*, October 22, 2005. http://www.jsonline.com/story/index.aspx?id=364891

———. "Life of the Party." JSOnline.com, *Milwaukee Journal Sentinel*, September 17, 2005. http://www.jsonline.com/story/index.aspx?id=356600

———. "Raised on Grit." JSOnline, *Milwaukee Journal Sentinel*, September 22, 2005. http://www.jsonline.com/story/index.aspx?id=355010

ESPN.com: "Favre Says He's Leaning Toward Retirement." January 30, 2006. http://sports.espn.go.com/nfl/news/story?id=2311729

Favre, Brett, and Chris Havel. *Favre: For the Record.* New York: Doubleday, 1997.

Flanigan, Kathy. "Deanna Favre Looks Back, Ahead." JSOnline, *Milwaukee Journal Sentinel*, October 5, 2005. http://www.jsonline.com/story/index.aspx?id=361176

Jones, Al. "Exclusive: Favre Indicates He Will Play an 18th Season at Green Bay." *SunHerald.com*, January 10, 2008. http://www.sunherald.com/news/breaking_news/story/292105.html

King, Peter. "Merely Human." *Sports Illustrated*, February 2, 1998. http://sportsillustrated.cnn.com/features/1998/weekly/980202/superbowlsb2.html

Miles, Jonathan. "#1 Best Job in America." *Men's Journal*, October 2005. http://www.mensjournal.com/feature/0510/brettFavre.html

Silverstein, Tom. "On My Terms." JSOnline.com, *Milwaukee Journal Sentinel*, March 7, 2008. http://www.officialbrettfavre.com/news/story_940075d2b9b2/

Vandermause, Mike. "Don't Shed a Tear: Expect Favre to Return." PackersNews.com, January 1, 2007. http://www.officialbrettfavre.com/news/story_347b8c6f0d61/

Weisman, Larry. "Deanna Favre Gives Green Bay Another Reason to Cheer." USA TODAY.com, October 19, 2005. http://www.usatoday.com/sports/football/nfl/packers/2005-10-19-deanna-favre-cover_x.htm

Yoder, Nathan, and David Thomason. "The Favres' Long Week." OfficialBrettFavre.com, October 31, 2004. http://www.officialbrettfavre.com/news/story_1930c12657467acf/

On the Internet

Brett Favre Fourward Foundation
http://www.officialbrettfavre.com/fourward_foundation/

Deanna Favre Hope Foundation
http://www.deannafavre4hope.com/

Official Brett Favre
http://www.officialbrettfavre.com

INDEX